Building a Peaceful School

Strategies and Interventions for Primary Schools

by Mollie Curry

A NASEN Publication

Published in 2001

ISBN 1 901485 20 X

The right of Mollie Curry to be identified as author of this work has been asserted by her in accordance with the Copyright, Designs and Patents Act 1988.

Published by NASEN.
NASEN is a company limited by guarantee, registered in England and Wales.
Company No. 2674379.
NASEN is a registered charity. Charity No. 1007023.

Further copies of this book and details of NASEN's many other publications may be obtained from the Publications Department at its registered office:
NASEN House, 4/5 Amber Business Village, Amber Close, Amington, Tamworth, Staffs. B77 4RP.
Tel: 01827 311500; Fax: 01827 313005
Email: welcome@nasen.org.uk; Website: www.nasen.org.uk

Copy editing by Nicola von Schreiber.
Cover design by Raphael Creative Design.
Typeset in Times by J. C. Typesetting and printed in the United Kingdom by Stowes (Stoke-on-Trent).

Contents

Acknowledgements

With thanks to Rosemary and Charlie for the drawings.

With thanks to St. Patrick's Cathedral, Dublin for permission to reproduce 'The Door of Reconciliation'.

Poems by Luke Welch reproduced with permission.

Introduction

This booklet seeks to find ways to build and maintain a peaceful school. Years ago it was more common to play outside of the home and there were many opportunities for mixed-aged friendships, as games passed from older to younger. Rules and expectations were learnt from other children, they experienced a variety of play environments, leading to a rich development of imaginative games.

Today's children may not be allowed the same freedoms. They may be more likely to have a structured leisure time in after-school activities or be passive participants of TV/computer. Parental concerns around safety can restrict spontaneity.

The school playground may be the only place to experience a sense of freedom and many children will need help to use their freedom in the playground, with friendships and playing harmoniously together.

The booklet aims to enhance the 'unstructured' time in primary schools. It seeks to give ways and means to include everyone in the process.

Conflicts are part of everyday living. Finding solutions can be healthy, creative and constructive. Not finding solutions can be stressful, immobilising and destructive. Adults and children both need to expand ways of resolution to build the peaceful school. Constructive approaches that reflect a willingness to listen, to understand and to explore ways to find mutual solutions from different perspectives enable children to see the benefit of rules, fairness and justice.

Resolutions of conflicts is a skill and can be taught. Resolutions enable a child to have a real choice about their behaviour and to be released from reproducing the same ineffective strategies that may result in aggression and hostility.

The responsibility to educate children in the understanding and experiences of citizenship is now upon schools. The school community needs to find ways to promote rules that focus on healthy options, so everyone can act responsibly within limits set by the rights and interests of others. The ideas found in this booklet will go a long way to develop children's life skills, values and attitudes, to add to their knowledge and understanding of themselves and awareness of others in an ethos of tolerance, justice and respect.

Children need to learn:

'to be able and willing to put aside self-interest and work with others for the common good'.

(QCA Draft Guidance - The Promotion of Pupils' Spiritual, Moral, Social and Cultural Development, November 1997)

Section One

Collecting data - examples/proforma

The Playground Book

Non-Violent Resolution

Prevention

Reparation

Circle-Time Activity

Resources

Collecting Data

Part of the routine in collecting data includes informing the children clearly and frequently about the expectations of their school on how ways can be found to 'be' together.

The emphasis is on safety, trust and respect. These are high ideals that need to be modelled and be part of the teacher's resolution style.

When school is usually a happy place for everyone there is an energy geared to prevention of conflict and a heightened awareness of other people and their perspectives.

Occasional surveys that monitor procedures and organisation of playgrounds are important, to keep a collective finger on the pulse.

Here are some examples and proforma on ways of gathering useful and relevant information. It is not suggested that all are used at once, but that teachers select appropriately to their current need.

Playground Data Collection - Finding out the children's view | A |

Name _____ Class _____
Where do you play at breaktime?
What do you usually do?
What do you like about breaktime?
What would you like to change about breaktime?
What are the problems for you?
This is confidential   Name: _____ *Thank You*

This could be a guide to whole class discussion or circle-time activity in Key Stage 1. In Key Stage 2 this could be individually completed.

Playground Data Collection - Staff perspective | B |

List main difficulties identified from the children's questionnaire.	
How do these things happen?	Why do they happen?
Which things can we deal with?	
Now	Later
Class	Year Group

The Playground Book

It is important for the adults in school to gain information and insight from the children about what is really going on. Use a playground book to have a regular system of reporting and recording incidents. This would involve the children in both identifying the problems from their perspective and in looking for short and long-term solutions.

Writing it down reflects the idea that everyone is working towards doing 'something' about their playground difficulties and that their voice is being heard.

The Playground Book

Names of those involved	
Date Time Place	Action taken By
Brief description	Outcome

Information from the Playground book can be used as reference points for work with individuals and/or groups.

Non-Violent Resolution

Children who experience difficulties in their peer and/or adult relationships can be helped by learning alternative ways of resolution. Fighting or physical aggression is often a habitual way of solving a problem albeit an inappropriate one.

Children need encouragement to experience alternatives thereby enabling them to understand what can be achieved and why the peaceful way is necessary. Aggression provides an immediate, momentary solution giving attention and prestige through physical power.

Non-violent problem solving may not be as exciting but is much more effective and thereby more rewarding long-term.

Well-managed conflict resolution gives the participants an experience of release.

Primary schools are in the position of being able to identify and work with young children who are showing aggressive tendencies as part of their peer group interaction. Efforts that are made to understand experiences and situations, to discuss and talk about feelings and their effect on behaviour, will add to a developing skill level. Aggression, if allowed to go on or inadvertently condoned by ignoring it, can escalate into something more serious at a later stage.

Preventative systems will help to gradually adjust the aggressive mindset. Work in small groups and individual input can sensitively but persistently enable appropriate problem-solving techniques to be assimilated. These pointers will help the adult when working with a child following an incident.

Think about...

- What is the underlying difficulty?
- How can their low self-esteem be actively raised in school?
- What do you think they were trying to do or communicate?
- Try to reach out and understand how it is for the aggressor.
- Understanding is not condoning but can help to find points of vulnerability.
- Children can be supported to learn to be assertive and to express needs safely.
- Start young!

In an ideal world, through peer conflicts children can be encouraged to understand what happened, so that the information can be transferred to other situations. Two ways of doing this can be achieved by 'putting things right' and by learning to avoid difficulties in the first place.

Successful conflict resolution puts the emphasis on *prevention* and *reparation*. Prevention is about empowering and skilling. Reparation is about attempts to make amends so victims feel 'heard' and everyone feel 'something was done'.

Prevention

Schools need to build and develop systems and structures that work to remove and inhibit aggression from the school culture.

- Involve children in playground management (see Responsibilities page 30).
- Organise active ongoing work on befriending and friendship skills (see page 35).
- Look at organisational issues about how large groups are moved around school.
- Welcome and befriend new children - not just for one or two days.
- Raise awareness by specific campaigns.
- Use circle-time to discuss problems and find solutions.
- Increase and widen repertoire of co-operative games
- Plan drama and role play scenarios with non-violent solutions composed by the children themselves.
- Involve parents.
- Look at long-term ways of improving the playground environment.
- Manage vigilant supervision bearing in mind most bullying occurs out of teachers' sight.
- Include language work during a peacemakers campaign (see page 19).
- Use stories to give another perspective.
- Promote art work for a poster campaign.
- Distribute surveys from time to time.
- Be alert for signs of distress.
- Revisit and refresh a class discussion on a definition of bullying. Always include verbal, non-verbal as well as physical harassment.

Finally, in schools where there is a conflict between the 'macho' culture of the home environment, 'my dad says if someone decks you, you hit them. No one's going to push me around', the response is 'here things are different. In school we do things in a different way.'

Reparation

This is an important ingredient in building a peaceful school ethos. For some children, unfortunately, 'sorry' is not enough and may even be meaningless. Adults can involve the children by:

- Asking - How can we put this right?
            - How can we make amends?
            - What can you do now about this?

And be ready to offer ideas about options by:

- Emphasising the importance of everyone's safety in school.
- Filling in a 'sorry sheet' or enter into the Playground Book (page 9).
- Praising and acknowledging children who 'own up' and accept responsibility for what has happened.
- Using circle-time to glean ideas from the children.
- Showing that reparation can be healing and helpful to a child learning peaceful ways of resolution.

The Door of Reconciliation

ST. PATRICK'S CATHEDRAL, DUBLIN

In 1492, two prominent families, the Ormonds and Kildares, were in the midst of a bitter feud. Besieged by Gerald Fitzgerald Earl of Kildare, Sir James Butler, Earl of Ormond, and his followers took refuge in the character house of St. Patrick's Cathedral, bolting themselves in. As the siege wore on, the Earl of Kildare concluded that the feuding was foolish. Here were two families worshipping the same God, in the same church, living in the same country, trying to kill each other. So he called out to Sir James and, as an inscription in St. Patrick's says today, "undertooke on his honour that he should receive no villanie".

Wary of "some further treacherie", Ormond did not respond. So Kildare seized his spear, cut away a hole in the door and thrust his hand through. It was grasped by another hand inside the church, the door was opened and the two men embraced, thus ending the family feud.

The expression "chancing one's arm" originated with Kildare's noble gesture. There is a lesson here for all of us who are engaged in "family feuds", whether brother to brother, language to language, nation to nation. If one of us would dare to "chance his arm", perhaps that would be the first crucial step to the reconciliation we all unconsciously seek.

Circle-Time Activity

TEASING - What happens when people start picking on us? Work in pairs - then whole group.

At playtime I don't like it when I get teased about …

What could we say or do when it happens?

What should we do if we see something being teased?

Reparation

How can you 'put things right'?

I am sorry that I …

I am going to try to …

To _____

From _____

Help Yourself

I know the feeling of torture
When no-one understands
Your parents want to help so much
But they can't
And it's annoying.

Wherever you go, you feel trapped
You can't seem to find a way out.
Yes, I've been there
Feeling the whole world is against me
Sensing that sometimes it really is.
But now I use these emotions - positive and negative
And you can too
As your determination grows
To battle through life and learn to love again

You can let the bully still believe you're nothing
While inside you know different
Which means
That soon
He will too

Luke Welch

Luke Welch has written a selection of poems on the theme of bullying. These can be discussion starters, or a stimulus for art or drama.

Resources

Curry, M. and Bromfield, C. (1994) *Positive Playtimes*. B.S.T. (available from 97 Heavitree Road, Exeter EX1 2NE).

Drew, N. (1987) *Learning the Skills of Peacemaking*. Jalmar Press: California.

Liebmann, M. (Ed.) (1996) *Arts Approaches to Conflict*. Jessica Kingsley: London.

Morse, P. S. and Ivey, A. E. (1996) *Face to Face,* Corwin Press: California.

NAPCE, c/o Institute of Education, University of Warwick, Coventry CV4 7AL.

QCA Draft Guidance - The Promotion of Pupils' Spiritual, Moral, Social and Cultural Development, November 1997.

Section Two

The Bullying Triangle

Bullying Questionnaire

Whole School Initiatives

Resources

The Bullying Triangle

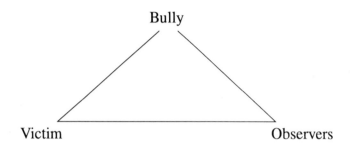

Bully

Victim   Observers

Bullying is a complex problem. When we begin to consider the possible causes, we soon realise that it is more than just the thrill of being powerful; it is also about attempts to redress a perceived lack of status, a low self-esteem, even fear and revenge. In efforts to manage and eradicate bullying from the school ethos there could be a tendency or temptation to repeat 'bullying' behaviour in responding to the bully. There are usually three components in a bullying situation, bully, victim and observer(s).

These bullying behaviours may be connected to children's early experiences, including a learned model of interaction, aggressive problem-solving strategies. This anti-social model can be changed and modified by early effective intervention in school before these patterns of behaviour become too entrenched.

Bullying Questionnaire

What are the things you enjoy about school? _____

_____

What are the things that bother you?_____

_____

_____

_____

_____

Do you know if there is any bullying going on?_____

_____

Who to? _____

_____

Who bullies? _____

_____

_____

Have you told anyone? _____

_____

_____

Where have you seen bullying?_____

_____

_____

Write here anything that happens to you in or out of class that upsets you _____

_____

_____

_____

_____

_____

Is there anything else you'd like to say? _____

_____

_____

Name _____   Class_____

This is confidential

This could be used at Key Stage 2 as part of a whole school initiative on bullying.

Whole School Initiatives

Schools can organise 'anti-bullying' campaigns from time to time. Incorporate art, literacy (see poems).

On a day-to-day basis they can encourage the following:

- Devise a mechanism for reporting incidents - especially the observers.
- A safe message box in each class.
- Confidentiality ensured.
- Frequent reminders of the adults' concern and desire to 'do something'.
- Encourage children to speak out or intervene if safe to do so.
- Organise buddies for the youngest, or children with special needs.
- Have a group of befrienders for newcomers over the first few weeks.
- Learn ways of resisting peer pressure to join in.
- Give attention to the 'injured' child first.
- Say it's okay to ask for help.

Bullying can be experienced in many ways. Nathan describes his feeling of rejection below. He had short hair which grew straight up - 'Nest cut' was a nickname.

Four eyes, nest cut, goody goody are the chants that are my routine everyday, I feel upset that no one likes me everyone teases me and most of all people hurt me. There are two main reasons that they tease me about but I'm so, so frustrated I'm still human not from mars. The first reason is that I am good at work as some people would say a goody goody I have tried getting my work wrong on purpose but then I just get told off by a teacher. The second reason is that I am bad at sport I do try to get better but no one passes to me or even lets me play. I feel left out all the time.

Nathan (Aged 8)

Resources

Broadwood, J., Langley, G. and Carmichael, H. *Promoting Positive Behaviour - Activities for Preventing Bullying in Primary Schools.* Headstart.

Smith, P. and Thomson, D. (1995) *Practical Approaches to Bullying.* David Fulton Publishers: London.

The Woodcraft Folk (1996) *Games Games Games.*

Reducing School Bullying - What works - Sonia Sharp
Available from NAPCE Base
c/o Institute of Education
University of Warwick
Coventry CV4 7AL

Video - *Walking on the Moon* (1999) available from:
Community Liaison Unit
Meridian Broadcasting
Television Centre
Southampton SO14 6PZ
Information pack is free

CD-ROMs - Primary and Secondary available from:
Coping with Life
P.O. Box 40
Ashington
NE63 8YR

WEBSITES
http://www.scre.ac.uk/bully/
http://www.bbc.co.uk/education/bully

Section Three

The Resolution Wheel

Modes of Resolution

Learning to Be Assertive

Negotiation

Mediation

Resources

The Resolution Wheel

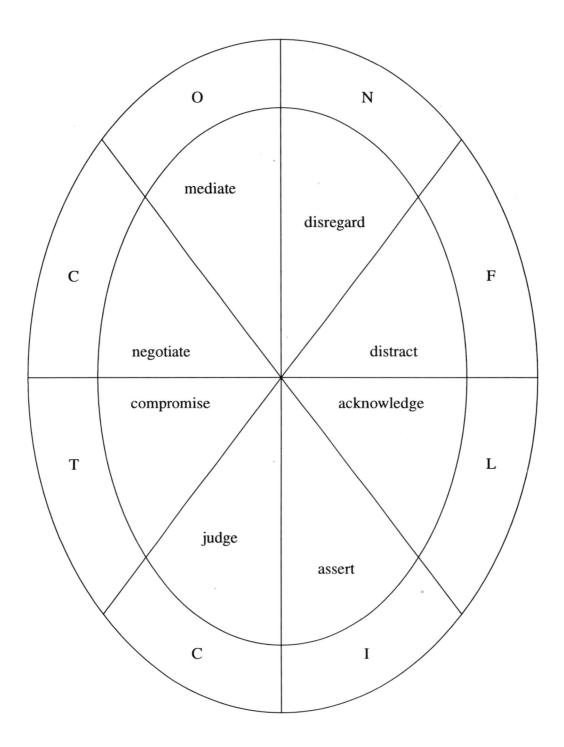

Successful resolution of conflicts is when both parties feel that they have been heard and go away with a sense of having their needs met. It can be seen as a gradual and growing developmental skill. This skill needs to be taught and practised in order for it to become a natural part of a child's repertoire.

Adults too can extend their skills by widening their choice of approach. Many conflicts that are repeated over and over again can be inhibited and even stopped by changing the way they are handled.

Conflicts are best tackled if:

- The audience is removed.
- Body language is not threatening.
- The tone of voice is calm.
- The child is not 'backed into a corner'.
- Options are available.
- There is time and space made to calm down if necessary.
- No unrealistic threats are made.
- Adults model the 'peacemakers' approach.

Teachers who widen their scope and modes of resolution will also expand the children's skills and awareness.

Modes of Resolution

Disregard	Distract
Ignoring inappropriate behaviour can be inhibiting. It works well when used positively, eg giving positive attention to the child who is nearby and who is behaving well. In the playground, walking away from difficulties is a first step to the child beginning to take responsibility for themselves. However, the perpetrator may be unaware of distress caused.	Young children can be diverted from inappropriate situations by refocusing their attention on to something or someone else. Difficult situations can be diffused in this way. As children get older this is less effective as not being able to express their viewpoint may lead to resentment.
Acknowledge	**Assert**
Children can feel supported by an adult acknowledging their sense of being upset by a playground difficulty. Their feelings are confirmed, and they have spoken to someone who has understood. The aggressor may be unaware - follow-up may be needed.	Children and adults are empowered by learning to express their feelings and having the opportunity to voice the effect of an inappropriate behaviour. The perpetrator receives information and the connection is made between the action and the consequence. Being assertive requires practice until it is absorbed fully (see page 24).
Judge	**Compromise**
The adult directly intervenes, usually by reminding the children of the school rule(s). There is no consideration of feelings or perceptions. The adult will usually give a clear message about what is right or wrong. Sanction or reparation may follow.	In a climate of creative and active resolution a compromise is possible. Each child will be expected to 'give' a little, or to take turns or share something. Compromise can be fraught with resentment if children are not fully involved in reaching it.
Negotiate	**Mediate**
Sometimes negotiation can be a misnomer for a bargaining 'deal' that children involve adults in. Negotiation is a skilled and structured operation. It requires time and energy and a degree of commitment on both sides. Once an agreement has been reached a time is set to review and evaluate its effectiveness.	Mediation involves two other people who act as mediators, one for each party. Mediators need to be trained, good listeners and able to retain confidentiality. Creative brainstorming helps to find solutions. It is a way of establishing appropriate ways of being together and to make a fresh start (see page 26).

23

Learning to Be Assertive

Children can be taught to express their needs and feelings in a way that is acceptable and respectful.

Assertiveness enables the points of disagreement or tension to be identified and for each person to be assisted to work towards a mutually satisfactory resolution.

The first step in teaching children to be assertive is enhanced by support from the adult. For example, in the playground a child comes to complain that someone is interfering with their game. Check first that they have asked them to stop. Then accompany the aggrieved child back to speak to the perpetrator. Ask for the request to be repeated, 'I don't like it when you keep running through our game. Please stop.' The adult can then say 'Did you hear that? What did they say?' This is supportive and the message is reinforced.

Teaching points
- Be clear about the issue - one thing at a time.
- No blaming or accusations - use 'I' statements.
- Avoid assumptions about the other person's feelings or motives. Check each person has heard the other.
- Encourage looking and listening.
- Involve both in the outcome, which will be helpful in reducing the possibility of the incident being repeated.
- Teach children to say, 'No - I don't like that' to another child when the play becomes uncomfortable.

Examples: 'I don't like it when I'm left out of the game and the ball doesn't get passed to me,'

or

'When you keep chasing me I feel fed up as I can't play my game.'

Reframing can be part of being assertive
Sometimes on the playground or in the classroom a child's request is both reasonable and appropriate but the aggressive way it is being expressed is not. Teach children to reframe expressions of low-key anger or frustration by starting the sentence with 'I'.

'I have asked…'
'I would like…'

In other words, the request may be okay but the way it is being delivered is not.

Negotiation

Negotiation is not 'bargaining'. It's a way of learning to see both points of view.

- Separate the problem from the child (ie it's the behaviour that's difficult).
- Identify the common concerns of both people.
- Make a list of possible solutions. Talk about how other people manage it.
- Choose something and reach agreement.

Fix date and time to review.

For example, in order to prevent the other side getting the ball, Ash keeps kicking the ball over the fence. Everyone gets angry with him and Jo wants him 'banned'.

Separate the problem:
- It wastes time when Ash kicks the ball over the fence.
- Everyone is annoyed about waiting for the ball.

Common concerns:
- Jo and Ash both want play to continue.
- Jo and Ash both become angry with the situation.

List of possible solutions:
- Leave the game for five minutes, if you feel angry.
- Jo to shout 'keep back' when he sees Ash getting angry, or Ash shouts 'hang on' for Jo.

Chosen solution:
- Ask to change position.

Other people…
- Usually accept that sometimes their team loses.
- Won't blame us if we lose.
- Keep away from the fence.

Review on Monday with Mrs Reff (morning break).

Mediation

Mediation is structured
A time and place is set aside. Mediation or similar initiatives using children need a named adult to monitor and support. This person acts as a point of reference and responsibility.

A Structure of Mediation
Both sides follow this step by step. Mediators reflect accurately what is said each time. Both children are asked:

1. What happened? Give facts, specific, objective, information, be objective.
2. How do you feel about what happened?
3. What do you wish to happen? Be creative, imaginative, you can wave a magic wand or freewheel!
4. What could you really do that is practical, realistic and fair?

Example
Lev and Keri keep arguing about using the tennis racquet at lunch time. Lev says he never has a proper go and Keri says Lev keeps snatching the racquet from her.

Person A - Lev
What happened?
Keri signs out for the tennis racquet and ball everyday, then won't hand them up when her time is up.

How do you feel?
I feel fed up about it and feel she is keeping the tennis racquet all to herself and I'm getting really angry with her. It's not fair.

What do you wish to happen?
She should be stopped from playing or bring in her own racquet.

What could you really do?
It would be fairer to agree which days she can go first.

Person B - Keri
What happened?
Lev snatches the racquet off me while I'm still playing, takes the ball too sometimes and he stops the game.

How do you feel?
I feel he's picking on me, pushing me around when I've signed out for the equipment. It's still my go.

What do you wish to happen?
He should play football or volleyball so I can have the racquet.

What could you really do?
I could let him keep time check for me and I'll keep time check for him. That would be fairer, I suppose.

Resources

Curry, M. and Bromfield, C. (1994) *PSE for Primary Schools through Circle-time.* NASEN: Tamworth.

Morse, P. and Ivey, A. (1996) *Face to Face.* Corwin Press: California.

Stacey, H. and Robinson, P. (1997) *Let's Mediate.* Lucky Duck Publishing: Bristol.

Stanford, G. (1990) *Developing Effective Classroom Groups.* Acora Books: Bristol.

Kingston Friends Workshop Group - 78 Eden Street, Kingston on Thames, Surrey, KT1 1DJ.

Section Four

Initiatives in Class

Responsibility

Using Stories

Friendship Issues

PSHE in Circle-Time

Using the Curriculum in Circle-Time

Resources

Initiatives in Class

Moral development is now an integral part of the spiritual, moral, social and cultural curriculum in every school, and guidance is expected to be given on enabling children to take responsibility for their actions. Children are also having to learn to work towards a fair and just resolution, within an agreed code of behaviour.

This code is based on the belief that everyone has rights and responsibilities to behave within the code and as citizens of the school community, and to be accountable for their actions.

This section looks at ways of bringing these ideals into realistic topics in the classroom.

(QCA The Promotion of Pupils' Spiritual, Moral, Social and Cultural Development Draft Guidance. November 1997.)

Overall goal: 'The school aims to ensure that pupils leave the school with the will and the ability to play a full and productive role in society.'

Objectives at Key Stages 1 and 2

Knowledge and understanding: pupils know and understand that no community can run smoothly unless everybody puts aside self-interest for the common good.

Skills: pupils are developing the ability to discuss joint goals and plans with others, to negotiate fairly and to put aside self-interest for the common good.

Qualities and attitudes: pupils are acquiring and/or developing a social conscience, respect for the views of others and self-discipline.

These objectives translate into classroom initiatives adding to the building of a peacemaker's ethos.

Keep a record of the variety of playground initiatives undertaken and found to be effective. This is useful information to share with colleagues.

Year Group
*Responsibilities in School
Stories
Friendship Issues
PSHE Topics of Circle-Time

Examples of Responsibilities*

KS 1 Take care of each other Know rules of safety Keep quiet area free of litter Water outside planters
Playleaders for Reception/Year 1 (volunteers on a rota) Teach playground games Return play equipment each day Keep KS 1 library area tidy
KS 2 Playground buddies for 'special' children in Year 2 (volunteers on a rota) Check equipment in and out Keep entrance hall tidy Help to lay and clear tables at lunch
Leadership role in school Privileges earned/withdrawn Collect data on breaktime issues Playground management committee (Some schools have found careful pairing of a Reception child to Year 6 as a befriender very beneficial. This can be extended to being a 'reading partner' once a week.)

Responsibility

This could be a circle-time activity to look at the issue of responsibility. It would follow on work being done on rules, understanding and drawing up rules.

The children are divided into twos and threes to discuss this and record their findings.

Rules bring with them responsibilities. Everyone is helped to be safe and allowed fairness.

At school we have to:
(Talk about all the things we have to do in school. Record your findings.)

At home I have to:
(Talk about all the things we have to do at home. Record your findings.)

Conference: Are there any differences between home and school responsibility?

Who says we have to do these things?

Why do we do them?

```
[                                                                    ]
```

What else should we do?

```
[                                                                    ]
```

Why do we have to learn about responsibility?

```
[                                                                    ]
```

Should children have less or more responsibility?

```
[                                                                    ]
```

When, at school, should children's views be taken seriously?

```
[                                                                    ]
```

How could we do that?

```
[                                                                    ]
```

These questions can act as a prompt to aid the whole group discussion in the conference part of circle-time.

Using Stories

Examples of Stories - Use to illustrate parallel situations and outcomes. Build a library of titles as a school resource.

KS 1

The Huge Bag of Worries - MacDonald - Virginia Ironside - How to cope with worries.
Borka - John Burningham - Red Fox - Teasing and being lonely.
Something else - Kathryn Cave - Puffin - Being different and rejected.
Elmer - David McKee - Red Fox - Being different.
'The Lion and the Mouse' in *The Very Best of Aesop's Fables* - retold by Margaret Clark - The small and insignificant help the strong and powerful.

KS 2

The Big Kick - Rob Child - Young Corgi - Football conflict (a series).
Friend or Foe - Michael Morpurgo - Mammoth - Teasing and moral dilemma.
A Kestrel for a Knave - Barry Hines - Puffin - Loss, sibling bullying.
Oliver Twist - Charles Dickens - Ladybird - Right and wrong cruelty.
Gowie Corby Plays Chicken - Gere Kerring - Puffin - Bullying.
Why we got chucked out of the Inter Schools Conflict - David Ross - Puffin - Football competition.

Stories can be used to discuss meaning and empathy. Ask questions such as:

'What is making them unhappy?'
'What does the story mean?'
'What do you think they could do next?'

Identify the feelings of the characters, how they tackle a problem and engage others in a solution. Stories safely explore another viewpoint. Try and find parallels in school.

Friendship Issues

Many children's squabbles and upsets are caused by difficulties in friendship. It's useful to remind ourselves of why friendships are important.

Through friendship we learn how to work and get on with one another; we experience companionship and the pleasure of interests shared. Friends are a wonderful resource if we have a problem. The quality of our interpersonal relationships affects our life, from childhood right through to adulthood, both personally and at work. If we have the support and friendship of other people difficult times are more bearable and happy times more joyful. Positive relationships make us feel good about ourselves and promote psychological health. But some children do not acquire the skills of friendship easily or the model of interaction they have is not conducive to positivity. A common element in children with behaviour problems is that they also have low self-esteem.

There is a certain level of conceptual skill required to enable children to think through and understand another person's perspective or viewpoint, a necessary ingredient of friendship. The poem *Speak Out!* identifies how friends can support each other.

Speak Out!

Speak out
Learn to scream and shout
Give your teachers headaches
If that's what it takes

State that you're not the only one
And what you have to say has just begun
Find a comrade; start a riot
Make a stand, destroy the quiet

Help yourself by helping another
Find the truth by going undercover
Then speak out and out and out
Learn to scream; learn to shout!

Luke Welch

If a child has low self-esteem or a negative view of themselves it will prevent or inhibit them from looking outside themselves and there will be difficulties in acquiring and learning an appropriate level of social and friendship skills.

Self-esteem influences how a child makes and maintains friendships. A child with high self-esteem will be confident in their contacts with others, able to take risks, and 'bounce back' if there's a problem, disagreement or upset. Often their high self-esteem enables them to anticipate or detect potential difficulties developing in the first place. A child with low self-esteem will be unable to take risks, and is more likely to prejudge a situation and even elicit failure – self-fulfilling prophecies. They may react negatively if things go wrong. Failure to overcome problems will confirm feelings of inadequacy and lack of self-worth. They may be unable to express feelings, fearing disapproval or rejection. If feelings are denied over a long period, the child begins to lose a real sense of who they are. Many children try to dampen or deny feelings of rejection or exclusion and inhibit the acquisition of skills necessary for making, building and maintaining friends.

Friendship skills may need teaching and should not be left to chance. It is a developmental process; what 6 year-olds need and look for in friendship will be different from 10 and 11 year-olds.

Work with children on identifying ingredients for friendship, components that will break it, and ways to build and maintain relationships. It is a topic that needs to be revisited many times - once is not enough!

Examples of Friendship Initiatives

KS 1

Awareness of threesome - some support/intervention may be needed to reduce tension.
Keep groups as fluid as possible.
Plan to mix boys and girls working and playing together.
Use circle-time to promote friendship skills and awareness.
Keep boy/girl mix for responsibility.
Use befrienders from older Year 3 groups to support vulnerable children in Reception/Year 1.

KS 2

Circle of friends to help isolated children (see Resource list on page 42).
Attention to newcomers - befriending programme.
Promote problem solving to alleviate squabbles (see section 3).
Endorse respect for the individual.
Celebrate individual achievement.
Promote differences and share experiences and values - culture.
Preparations for transfer.

Activity for Circle-Time
This can be used with Reception, one section at a time, or as a whole from Year 1 upwards.

Work in twos and threes

What are friends for?
When do you most need a friend?
How can we be a friend?
Is there more to friendship than doing things together?

Use the information gleaned from circle-time to build up a bank of ideas. Celebrate success!

What do the observers do in a bullying situation? This poem describes their perspective.

Safety in Numbers

Maybe a cry for help isn't the best way to make friends
But it is the quickest way to label yourself.

'Oh, look at him,
Why don't he fight back?'
'Well, what do you expect?'
'Who is he anyway?'
'Some little twat from the first year.'

'Oh, yeah! The one from the other day
When it was pissing down
They pulled the guttering off the shed
And poured crap all over him.'

'What's he done to deserve this?'

'Dunno.'

'Did he say anything?'
'No, all he... Oh, look, he's crying.'
'He's shouting something.'
'Piss off, expected us to end up like him.'

'There's one thing though -
He can certainly take a beating.
Look, gotta go,
After school I'll walk back with you!'

'Right... Safer that way!'

Luke Welch

Activity for Circle-Time
Think of a problem you've had with a friend recently.

What helped it to be sorted out?	What stopped it being sorted out?

Photocopy and cut into four. Give one to each child. Emphasise this is confidential. This helps to organise seating plans.

Friendship Groups

Best Friend
Friend
A Working Partner
A Helpful Partner

Friendship Groups

Best Friend
Friend
A Working Partner
A Helpful Partner

Friendship Groups

Best Friend
Friend
A Working Partner
A Helpful Partner

Friendship Groups

Best Friend
Friend
A Working Partner
A Helpful Partner

PSHE in Circle-Time

Examples of PSHE Topics - providing a vehicle to raise concerns, in safety and to explore solutions.

KS 1

School expectations.
Friendships.
Listening.
Turn-taking.
Looking after each other.
Things that make me angry.
Fears.
Special days.

KS 2

Choices.
Resisting peer pressure.
How we can work together in groups.
Playground issues.
Managing anger.
Feelings.
Discrimination.
Responsibilities.
Image and kudos.

Using the Curriculum in Circle-Time

The Humanities Curriculum lends itself to many conflict situations. Pulling out the PSHE threads from topics enhances the cross-curricula links and connects attitudes and experience.

Here are some examples:
Invaders and settlers.

This theme lends itself to issues such as prejudice and reflection and to positive and negative influences from different cultures. Other topics like *loyalty, racism,* even *football teams* could be touched on if relevant.

Look at how conflicts between nations and peoples are resolved (or not) as these can provide pointers for discussion. This is a way of expanding issues from local or school-based to the more global, essential in terms of race/differences issues. Current affairs illustrate graphically national or 'tribal' bullying and the connections need to be made if individuals can collectively make a difference. Acquisition of knowledge awareness and skills are essential.

Here are four examples of a circle-time activity based on curriculum topics.

Circle-time - Activity A

Being a peacemaker
(Work in threes. Discuss each part and then record the findings. There would need to be a clarification on what a peacemaker is. This could be used from Year 4 upwards.)

What is a peacemaker?	How can we be peacemakers here in school?

This is how we could organise it

Circle-time - Activity B

Going to a new country
(Draw or write answers. Think about if you had to leave your home/country. Work with a partner or in threes. Think about why people have to move.)

Good feelings (in one colour)

Not good feelings (in another colour)

These might help us feel better...

Circle-time - Activity C

Leadership - Tudor - Henry VIII
(In groups of four choose a scribe and spokesperson.)

What kind of a king was Henry VIII?	
How do you feel about what he did?	What sort of person was he?
From this we can learn...	

Elicit from each group:
What kind of leader was he? Do you agree? Could he have found another way of ruling the country?

Circle-time - Activity D

Elizabeth 1
(What made Elizabeth a good queen? Think about how she was different from Henry. Write in each box.)

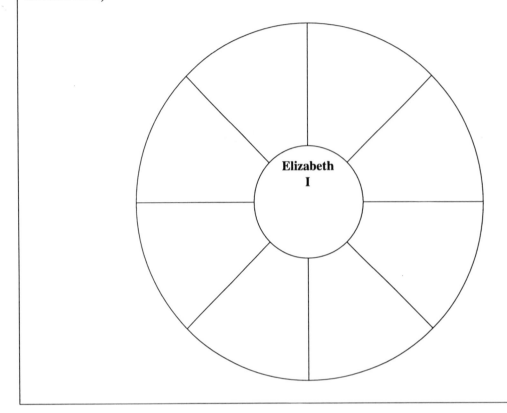

Resources

Fisher, R. (1996) *Stories for Thinking.* Nash Pollock Publishing: Oxford.

Newton, C. and Wilson, D. (1998) *Circles of Friends.* Folens Publishers.

Parkin, J. and Klein, R. (1999) 'The New Play Managers' in *TES* (07/05/1999).

Ross, C. (1997) *Something to Draw On.* Jessica Kingsley: London.

Welch, L. (1998) *Let it be said.* Chilli Pepper: Cambridge.

The Citizenship Foundation - 15 St. Swithins Lane, London, EC4 8AL. *Classroom Resources.*

I'm His Teacher

So many things to mark
Assignments to give out
Targets to reach
I see one lad's marks have slipped again
I've tried talking to him
He just looked back at me, as if he was lost
Of course it might be a family problem
His parents did explain that he was
Having trouble settling in
Yes, it's probably just a phase he's going through
And if it is really important
He could always come and talk to me
I'd like to help
You know I'd like to help.
But at the moment
As you can see
I'm a bit snowed under.

Luke Welch

Conclusion

The guidance for schools on the spiritual, moral, social and cultural development clearly states that children need to learn to value themselves, to value relationships, to value society and to value the environment.

Much of this can be achieved at primary level by facilitating the will and ability to be responsible, to care and co-operate with others, to acquire and practise skills, to form and sustain good relationships.

Healthy ways of resolution give the arena for all this. Participation and belonging go a long way to developing appropriate values, qualities and attitudes.

The skills and awareness that will contribute to the building of a peaceful school need practice, rehearsal and fine tuning, and to be driven at a pace that gives time for the skills to be absorbed.

Healthy resolution provides the area in which this can take place. Avoidance of resolution causes triangling, ie a third person colludes, takes sides, or maintains the conflict. Conflict creates an energy which when channelled makes change possible.

We can learn from the Samurai, the Japanese Sword Warriors, as they display absolute tenacity in their dedication to their skills.

'Japanese masters of the swords learn their skills through a set of highly detailed training exercises. The process of masterful swordsmanship is broken down into specific skills and studied carefully - one at a time.'

'Each single skill is practised until a fine point of mastery is achieved. Perfection and smoothness of execution is the goal. Once the Samurai complete their course of training, they retreat to a mountaintop to meditate and forget about the skills they have just learned. Upon returning to the lowlands, they have naturally integrated the skills into their being.'

'Excellence in education requires masterful communication: the ability to listen and learn, to focus and confront, and to lead and influence others. Critical to all these skills is mastery in the sense of the Samurai.'

(Morse (96) Face to Face)

Successful conflict resolution requires practice and understanding gradually leading to the acquisition of peacemaking skills.

We need to encourage our children to become masters of the art of peaceful resolution.